Cram101 Textbook Outlines to accompany:

Sales Forecasting Management:A Demand Management Approach

Mentzer, Moon, 2nd Edition

An Academic Internet Publishers (AIPI) publication (c) 2007.

You have a discounted membership at www.Cram101.com with this book.

Get all of the practice tests for the chapters of this textbook, and access in-depth reference material for writing essays and papers. Here is an example from a Cram101 Biology text:

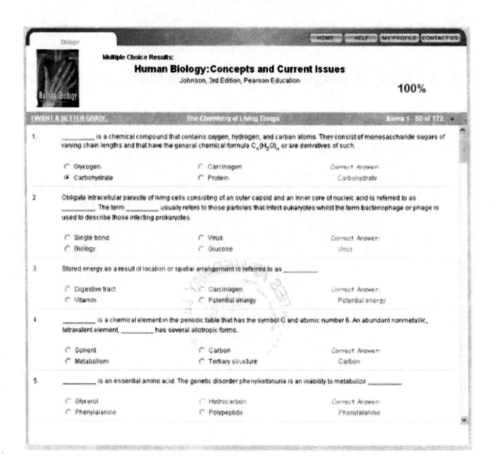

When you need problem solving help with math, stats, and other disciplines, www.Cram101.com will walk through the formulas and solutions step by step.

With Cram101.com online, you also have access to extensive reference material.

You will nail those essays and papers. Here is an example from a Cram101 Biology text:

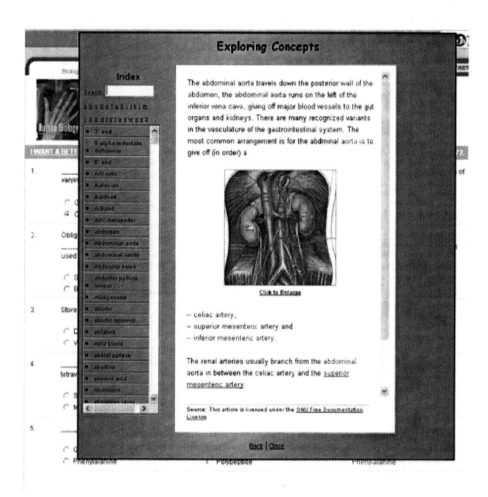

Learning System

Cram101 Textbook Outlines is a learning system. The notes in this book are the highlights of your textbook, you will never have to highlight a book again.

How to use this book. Take this book to class, it is your notebook for the lecture. The notes and highlights on the left hand side of the pages follow the outline and order of the textbook. All you have to do is follow along while your intructor presents the lecture. Circle the items emphasized in class and add other important information on the right side. With Cram101 Textbook Outlines you'll spend less time writing and more time listening. Learning becomes more efficient.

Cram101.com Online

Increase your studying efficiency by using Cram101.com's practice tests and online reference material. It is the perfect complement to Cram101 Textbook Outlines. Use self-teaching matching tests or simulate in-class testing with comprehensive multiple choice tests, or simply use Cram's true and false tests for quick review. Cram101.com even allows you to enter your in-class notes for an integrated studying format combining the textbook notes with your class notes.

Visit **www.Cram101.com**, click Sign Up at the top of the screen, and enter **DK73DW3455** in the promo code box on the registration screen. Access to www.Cram101.com is normally $9.95, but because you have purchased this book, your access fee is only $4.95. Sign up and stop highlighting textbooks forever.

Sales Forecasting Management:A Demand Management Approach
Mentzer, Moon, 2nd

CONTENTS

Supply chain	Supply chain refers to the flow of goods, services, and information from the initial sources of materials and services to the delivery of products to consumers.
Outsourcing	Outsourcing refers to a production activity that was previously done inside a firm or plant that is now conducted outside that firm or plant.
Procurement	Procurement is the acquisition of goods or services at the best possible total cost of ownership, in the right quantity, at the right time, in the right place for the direct benefit or use of the governments, corporations, or individuals generally via, but not limited to a contract.
Production	The creation of finished goods and services using the factors of production: land, labor, capital, entrepreneurship, and knowledge.
Operation	A standardized method or technique that is performed repetitively, often on different materials resulting in different finished goods is called an operation.
Inventory	Tangible property held for sale in the normal course of business or used in producing goods or services for sale is an inventory.
Overtime	Overtime is the amount of time someone works beyond normal working hours.
Supply	Supply is the aggregate amount of any material good that can be called into being at a certain price point; it comprises one half of the equation of supply and demand. In classical economic theory, a curve representing supply is one of the factors that produce price.
Margin	A deposit by a buyer in stocks with a seller or a stockbroker, as security to cover fluctuations in the market in reference to stocks that the buyer has purchased but for which he has not paid is a margin. Commodities are also traded on margin.
Spot market	Spot market refers to a market in which commodities are bought and sold for cash and immediate delivery.
Market	A market is, as defined in economics, a social arrangement that allows buyers and sellers to discover information and carry out a voluntary exchange of goods or services.
Policy	Similar to a script in that a policy can be a less than completely rational decision-making method. Involves the use of a pre-existing set of decision steps for any problem that presents itself.
Derived demand	Derived demand refers to demand that arises or is defined indirectly from some other demand or underlying behavior.
Discount	The difference between the face value of a bond and its selling price, when a bond is sold for less than its face value it's referred to as a discount.
Total demand	Total demand refers to the demand schedule or the demand curve of all buyers of a good or service; also called market demand.
Safety stock	Safety stock is additional inventory planned to buffer against the variability in supply and demand plans, that could otherwise result in inventory shortages.
Stock	In financial terminology, stock is the capital raized by a corporation, through the issuance and sale of shares.
Sales forecasting	Sales forecasting refers to the process of predicting sales of services or goods. The initial step in preparing a master budget.
Management	Management characterizes the process of leading and directing all or part of an organization, often a business, through the deployment and manipulation of resources. Early twentieth-century management writer Mary Parker Follett defined management as "the art of getting things done through people."
Demand management	The use of fiscal policy and monetary policy to increase or decrease aggregate demand is called demand management.

Consumption	In Keynesian economics consumption refers to personal consumption expenditure, i.e., the purchase of currently produced goods and services out of income, out of savings (net worth), or from borrowed funds. It refers to that part of disposable income that does not go to saving.
Business operations	Business operations are those activities involved in the running of a business for the purpose of producing value for the stakeholders. The outcome of business operations is the harvesting of value from assets owned by a business.
Purchasing	Purchasing refers to the function in a firm that searches for quality material resources, finds the best suppliers, and negotiates the best price for goods and services.
Bill of materials	A bill of materials describes a product in terms of its assemblies, sub-assemblies, and basic parts. Basically consisting of a list of parts, a bill of materials is an essential part of the design and manufacture of any product.
Bill of material	A bill of material is a list of all the materials needed to manufacture a product or product component.
Service	Service refers to a "non tangible product" that is not embodied in a physical good and that typically effects some change in another product, person, or institution. Contrasts with good.
Customer service	The ability of logistics management to satisfy users in terms of time, dependability, communication, and convenience is called the customer service.
Raw material	Raw material refers to a good that has not been transformed by production; a primary product.
Contribution	In business organization law, the cash or property contributed to a business by its owners is referred to as contribution.
Assessment	Collecting information and providing feedback to employees about their behavior, communication style, or skills is an assessment.
Marketing	Promoting and selling products or services to customers, or prospective customers, is referred to as marketing.
Profit	Profit refers to the return to the resource entrepreneurial ability; total revenue minus total cost.
Supply chain management	Supply chain management deals with the planning and execution issues involved in managing a supply chain. Supply chain management spans all movement and storage of raw materials, work-in-process inventory, and finished goods from point-of-origin to point-of-consumption.
Context	The effect of the background under which a message often takes on more and richer meaning is a context. Context is especially important in cross-cultural interactions because some cultures are said to be high context or low context.
Users	Users refer to people in the organization who actually use the product or service purchased by the buying center.
Information system	An information system is a system whether automated or manual, that comprises people, machines, and/or methods organized to collect, process, transmit, and disseminate data that represent user information.
Sales forecast	Sales forecast refers to the maximum total sales of a product that a firm expects to sell during a specified time period under specified environmental conditions and its own marketing efforts.
Contract	A contract is a "promise" or an "agreement" that is enforced or recognized by the law. In the civil law, a contract is considered to be part of the general law of obligations.
Manufacturing	Production of goods primarily by the application of labor and capital to raw materials and other intermediate inputs, in contrast to agriculture, mining, forestry, fishing, and services a manufacturing.
Firm	An organization that employs resources to produce a good or service for profit and owns and operates one or more plants is referred to as a firm.

Industry	A group of firms that produce identical or similar products is an industry. It is also used specifically to refer to an area of economic production focused on manufacturing which involves large amounts of capital investment before any profit can be realized, also called "heavy industry".
Profit plan	A comprehensive set of budgets that cover all phases of an organization's operations during a specified period of time is called a profit plan.
Personnel	A collective term for all of the employees of an organization. Personnel is also commonly used to refer to the personnel management function or the organizational unit responsible for administering personnel programs.
Management functions	Management functions were set forth by Henri Fayol; they include planning, organizing, leading, and controling.
Variance	Variance refers to a measure of how much an economic or statistical variable varies across values or observations. Its calculation is the same as that of the covariance, being the covariance of the variable with itself.
Quota	A government-imposed restriction on quantity, or sometimes on total value, used to restrict the import of something to a specific quantity is called a quota.
Mistake	In contract law a mistake is incorrect understanding by one or more parties to a contract and may be used as grounds to invalidate the agreement. Common law has identified three different types of mistake in contract: unilateral mistake, mutual mistake, and common mistake.
Matching	Matching refers to an accounting concept that establishes when expenses are recognized. Expenses are matched with the revenues they helped to generate and are recognized when those revenues are recognized.
Enterprise	Enterprise refers to another name for a business organization. Other similar terms are business firm, sometimes simply business, sometimes simply firm, as well as company, and entity.
Wholesale	According to the United Nations Statistics Division Wholesale is the resale of new and used goods to retailers, to industrial, commercial, institutional or professional users, or to other wholesalers, or involves acting as an agent or broker in buying merchandise for, or selling merchandise, to such persons or companies.
Channel	Channel, in communications (sometimes called communications channel), refers to the medium used to convey information from a sender (or transmitter) to a receiver.
Distribution	Distribution in economics, the manner in which total output and income is distributed among individuals or factors.
Logistics	Those activities that focus on getting the right amount of the right products to the right place at the right time at the lowest possible cost is referred to as logistics.
Human resources	Human resources refers to the individuals within the firm, and to the portion of the firm's organization that deals with hiring, firing, training, and other personnel issues.
Planning horizon	The length of time it takes to conceive, develop, and complete a project and to recover the cost of the project on a discounted cash flow basis is referred to as planning horizon.
Time horizon	A time horizon is a fixed point of time in the future at which point certain processes will be evaluated or assumed to end. It is necessary in an accounting, finance or risk management regime to assign such a fixed horizon time so that alternatives can be evaluated for performance over the same period of time.
Hierarchy	A system of grouping people in an organization according to rank from the top down in which all subordinate managers must report to one person is called a hierarchy.
Corporation	A legal entity chartered by a state or the Federal government that is distinct and separate from the

Go to **Cram101.com** for the Practice Tests for this Chapter.

individuals who own it is a corporation. This separation gives the corporation unique powers which other legal entities lack.

Product line	A group of products that are physically similar or are intended for a similar market are called the product line.
Marketing Plan	Marketing plan refers to a road map for the marketing activities of an organization for a specified future period of time, such as one year or five years.
Sales management	Planning the selling program and implementing and controlling the personal selling effort of the firm is called sales management.
Accounting	A system that collects and processes financial information about an organization and reports that information to decision makers is referred to as accounting.
Capital	Capital generally refers to financial wealth, especially that used to start or maintain a business. In classical economics, capital is one of four factors of production, the others being land and labor and entrepreneurship.
Stock keeping unit	Stock keeping unit refers to a unique identification number that defines an item for ordering or inventory purposes.
Time series	In statistics and signal processing, a time series is a sequence of data points, measured typically at successive times, spaced at (often uniform) time intervals. Analysts throughout the economy will use these to aid in the management of their corresponding businesses.
Trend	Trend refers to the long-term movement of an economic variable, such as its average rate of increase or decrease over enough years to encompass several business cycles.
Complexity	The technical sophistication of the product and hence the amount of understanding required to use it is referred to as complexity. It is the opposite of simplicity.
Smoothing	That which involves playing down differences and finding areas of agreement are referred to as accommodation or smoothing.
Correlation	A correlation is the measure of the extent to which two economic or statistical variables move together, normalized so that its values range from -1 to +1. It is defined as the covariance of the two variables divided by the square root of the product of their variances.
Advertising	Advertising refers to paid, nonpersonal communication through various media by organizations and individuals who are in some way identified in the advertising message.
Variable	A variable is something measured by a number; it is used to analyze what happens to other things when the size of that number changes.
Economy	The income, expenditures, and resources that affect the cost of running a business and household are called an economy.
Exogenous variable	Exogenous variable refers to a variable that is taken as given by an economic model. It therefore is subject to direct manipulation by the modeler. In most models, policy variables such as tariffs and par values of pegged exchange rates are exogenous.
Committee	A long-lasting, sometimes permanent team in the organization structure created to deal with tasks that recur regularly is the committee.
Technology	The body of knowledge and techniques that can be used to combine economic resources to produce goods and services is called technology.
Information technology	Information technology refers to technology that helps companies change business by allowing them to use new methods.
Warehouse	Warehouse refers to a location, often decentralized, that a firm uses to store, consolidate, age, or

9

mix stock; house product-recall programs; or ease tax burdens.

Data warehouse	A Data warehouse is a repository of integrated information, available for queries and analysis. Data and information are extracted from heterogeneous sources as they are generated.
Exchange	The trade of things of value between buyer and seller so that each is better off after the trade is called the exchange.
Protocol	Protocol refers to a statement that, before product development begins, identifies a well-defined target market; specific customers' needs, wants, and preferences; and what the product will be and do.
Collaboration	Collaboration occurs when the interaction between groups is very important to goal attainment and the goals are compatible. Wherein people work together —applying both to the work of individuals as well as larger collectives and societies.
Integration	Economic integration refers to reducing barriers among countries to transactions and to movements of goods, capital, and labor, including harmonization of laws, regulations, and standards. Integrated markets theoretically function as a unified market.
Brand	A name, symbol, or design that identifies the goods or services of one seller or group of sellers and distinguishes them from the goods and services of competitors is a brand.
Negotiation	Negotiation is the process whereby interested parties resolve disputes, agree upon courses of action, bargain for individual or collective advantage, and/or attempt to craft outcomes which serve their mutual interests.
Aid	Assistance provided by countries and by international institutions such as the World Bank to developing countries in the form of monetary grants, loans at low interest rates, in kind, or a combination of these is called aid. Aid can also refer to assistance of any type rendered to benefit some group or individual.
Direct sale	A direct sale is a sale to customers through distributors or self-employed sales people rather than through shops. Includes both personal contact with consumers in their homes (and other nonstore locations such as offices) and phone solicitations initiated by a retailer.
Promotion	Promotion refers to all the techniques sellers use to motivate people to buy products or services. An attempt by marketers to inform people about products and to persuade them to participate in an exchange.
Invoice	The itemized bill for a transaction, stating the nature of the transaction and its cost. In international trade, the invoice price is often the preferred basis for levying an ad valorem tariff.
Credibility	The extent to which a source is perceived as having knowledge, skill, or experience relevant to a communication topic and can be trusted to give an unbiased opinion or present objective information on the issue is called credibility.
Budget	Budget refers to an account, usually for a year, of the planned expenditures and the expected receipts of an entity. For a government, the receipts are tax revenues.
Investment	Investment refers to spending for the production and accumulation of capital and additions to inventories. In a financial sense, buying an asset with the expectation of making a return.
Business plan	A detailed written statement that describes the nature of the business, the target market, the advantages the business will have in relation to competition, and the resources and qualifications of the owner is referred to as a business plan.

Allowance	Reduction in the selling price of goods extended to the buyer because the goods are defective or of lower quality than the buyer ordered and to encourage a buyer to keep merchandise that would otherwise be returned is the allowance.
Management	Management characterizes the process of leading and directing all or part of an organization, often a business, through the deployment and manipulation of resources. Early twentieth-century management writer Mary Parker Follett defined management as "the art of getting things done through people."
Sales forecasting	Sales forecasting refers to the process of predicting sales of services or goods. The initial step in preparing a master budget.
Sales forecast	Sales forecast refers to the maximum total sales of a product that a firm expects to sell during a specified time period under specified environmental conditions and its own marketing efforts.
Operation	A standardized method or technique that is performed repetitively, often on different materials resulting in different finished goods is called an operation.
Marketing	Promoting and selling products or services to customers, or prospective customers, is referred to as marketing.
Market	A market is, as defined in economics, a social arrangement that allows buyers and sellers to discover information and carry out a voluntary exchange of goods or services.
Customer satisfaction	Customer satisfaction is a business term which is used to capture the idea of measuring how satisfied an enterprise's customers are with the organization's efforts in a marketplace.
Supply chain	Supply chain refers to the flow of goods, services, and information from the initial sources of materials and services to the delivery of products to consumers.
Supply	Supply is the aggregate amount of any material good that can be called into being at a certain price point; it comprises one half of the equation of supply and demand. In classical economic theory, a curve representing supply is one of the factors that produce price.
Yield	The interest rate that equates a future value or an annuity to a given present value is a yield.
Distortion	Distortion refers to any departure from the ideal of perfect competition that interferes with economic agents maximizing social welfare when they maximize their own.
Time horizon	A time horizon is a fixed point of time in the future at which point certain processes will be evaluated or assumed to end. It is necessary in an accounting, finance or risk management regime to assign such a fixed horizon time so that alternatives can be evaluated for performance over the same period of time.
Production	The creation of finished goods and services using the factors of production: land, labor, capital, entrepreneurship, and knowledge.
Service	Service refers to a "non tangible product" that is not embodied in a physical good and that typically effects some change in another product, person, or institution. Contrasts with good.
Customer service	The ability of logistics management to satisfy users in terms of time, dependability, communication, and convenience is called the customer service.
Investment	Investment refers to spending for the production and accumulation of capital and additions to inventories. In a financial sense, buying an asset with the expectation of making a return.
Return on investment	Return on investment refers to the return a businessperson gets on the money he and other owners invest in the firm; for example, a business that earned $100 on a $1,000 investment

Go to **Cram101.com** for the Practice Tests for this Chapter.

would have a ROI of 10 percent: 100 divided by 1000.

Marketing cost	Marketing cost refers to the cost incurred in selling goods or services. Includes order-getting costs and order-filling or distribution costs.
Personnel	A collective term for all of the employees of an organization. Personnel is also commonly used to refer to the personnel management function or the organizational unit responsible for administering personnel programs.
Variable	A variable is something measured by a number; it is used to analyze what happens to other things when the size of that number changes.
Staffing	Staffing refers to a management function that includes hiring, motivating, and retaining the best people available to accomplish the company's objectives.
Expense	In accounting, an expense represents an event in which an asset is used up or a liability is incurred. In terms of the accounting equation, expenses reduce owners' equity.
Aftermarket	The market for a new security offering immediately after it is sold to the public is referred to as aftermarket.
Time series	In statistics and signal processing, a time series is a sequence of data points, measured typically at successive times, spaced at (often uniform) time intervals. Analysts throughout the economy will use these to aid in the management of their corresponding businesses.
Users	Users refer to people in the organization who actually use the product or service purchased by the buying center.
Budget	Budget refers to an account, usually for a year, of the planned expenditures and the expected receipts of an entity. For a government, the receipts are tax revenues.
Logistics	Those activities that focus on getting the right amount of the right products to the right place at the right time at the lowest possible cost is referred to as logistics.
Mistake	In contract law a mistake is incorrect understanding by one or more parties to a contract and may be used as grounds to invalidate the agreement. Common law has identified three different types of mistake in contract: unilateral mistake, mutual mistake, and common mistake.
Raw material	Raw material refers to a good that has not been transformed by production; a primary product.
Inventory	Tangible property held for sale in the normal course of business or used in producing goods or services for sale is an inventory.
Finished goods	Completed products awaiting sale are called finished goods. An item considered a finished good in a supplying plant might be considered a component or raw material in a receiving plant.
Market share	That fraction of an industry's output accounted for by an individual firm or group of firms is called market share.
Competitor	Other organizations in the same industry or type of business that provide a good or service to the same set of customers is referred to as a competitor.
Promotion	Promotion refers to all the techniques sellers use to motivate people to buy products or services. An attempt by marketers to inform people about products and to persuade them to participate in an exchange.
Balance	In banking and accountancy, the outstanding balance is the amount of money owned, (or due), that remains in a deposit account (or a loan account) at a given date, after all past remittances, payments and withdrawal have been accounted for. It can be positive (then, in the balance sheet of a firm, it is an asset) or negative (a liability).

Balance sheet	A statement of the assets, liabilities, and net worth of a firm or individual at some given time often at the end of its "fiscal year," is referred to as a balance sheet.
Industry	A group of firms that produce identical or similar products is an industry. It is also used specifically to refer to an area of economic production focused on manufacturing which involves large amounts of capital investment before any profit can be realized, also called "heavy industry".
Quota	A government-imposed restriction on quantity, or sometimes on total value, used to restrict the import of something to a specific quantity is called a quota.
Contribution	In business organization law, the cash or property contributed to a business by its owners is referred to as contribution.
Advertising	Advertising refers to paid, nonpersonal communication through various media by organizations and individuals who are in some way identified in the advertising message.
Profit	Profit refers to the return to the resource entrepreneurial ability; total revenue minus total cost.
Product development	In business and engineering, new product development is the complete process of bringing a new product to market. There are two parallel aspects to this process : one involves product engineering ; the other marketing analysis. Marketers see new product development as the first stage in product life cycle management, engineers as part of Product Lifecycle Management.
Distribution	Distribution in economics, the manner in which total output and income is distributed among individuals or factors.
Context	The effect of the background under which a message often takes on more and richer meaning is a context. Context is especially important in cross-cultural interactions because some cultures are said to be high context or low context.
Shareholder	A shareholder is an individual or company (including a corporation) that legally owns one or more shares of stock in a joined stock company.
Shareholder value	For a publicly traded company, shareholder value is the part of its capitalization that is equity as opposed to long-term debt. In the case of only one type of stock, this would roughly be the number of outstanding shares times current shareprice.
DuPont	DuPont was the inventor of CFCs (along with General Motors) and the largest producer of these ozone depleting chemicals (used primarily in aerosol sprays and refrigerants) in the world, with a 25% market share in the late 1980s.
Net assets	Net assets refers to portion of the assets remaining after the creditors' claims have been satisfied; also called equity or residual interest.
Capital	Capital generally refers to financial wealth, especially that used to start or maintain a business. In classical economics, capital is one of four factors of production, the others being land and labor and entrepreneurship.
Asset	An item of property, such as land, capital, money, a share in ownership, or a claim on others for future payment, such as a bond or a bank deposit is an asset.
Operating expense	In throughput accounting, the cost accounting aspect of Theory of Constraints (TOC), operating expense is the money spent turning inventory into throughput. In TOC, operating expense is limited to costs that vary strictly with the quantity produced, like raw materials and purchased components.
Revenue	Revenue is a U.S. business term for the amount of money that a company receives from its activities, mostly from sales of products and/or services to customers.

Gross margin	Gross margin is an ambiguous phrase that expresses the relationship between gross profit and sales revenue as Gross Margin = Revenue - costs of good sold.
Margin	A deposit by a buyer in stocks with a seller or a stockbroker, as security to cover fluctuations in the market in reference to stocks that the buyer has purchased but for which he has not paid is a margin. Commodities are also traded on margin.
Business unit	The lowest level of the company which contains the set of functions that carry a product through its life span from concept through manufacture, distribution, sales and service is a business unit.
Accounts receivable	Accounts receivable is one of a series of accounting transactions dealing with the billing of customers which owe money to a person, company or organization for goods and services that have been provided to the customer. This is typically done in a one person organization by writing an invoice and mailing or delivering it to each customer.
Retained earnings	Cumulative earnings of a company that are not distributed to the owners and are reinvested in the business are called retained earnings.
Total demand	Total demand refers to the demand schedule or the demand curve of all buyers of a good or service; also called market demand.
Carrying cost	The cost to hold an asset, usually inventory is called a carrying cost. For inventory, a carrying cost includes such items as interest, warehousing costs, insurance, and material-handling expenses.
Procurement	Procurement is the acquisition of goods or services at the best possible total cost of ownership, in the right quantity, at the right time, in the right place for the direct benefit or use of the governments, corporations, or individuals generally via, but not limited to a contract.
Incidence	The ultimate economic effect of a tax on the real incomes of producers or consumers. Thus a sales tax may be paid by a retailer, but it is likely that the incidence falls upon the consumer.
Distribution center	Designed to facilitate the timely movement of goods and represent a very important part of a supply chain is a distribution center.
Dividend	Amount of corporate profits paid out for each share of stock is referred to as dividend.
Working capital	The dollar difference between total current assets and total current liabilities is called working capital.
Fixed capital	Fixed capital is a concept in economics and accounting, first theoretically analysed in some depth by the economist David Ricardo. It refers to any kind of real or physical capital that is not used up in the production of a product. It is contrasted with circulating capital.
Demand management	The use of fiscal policy and monetary policy to increase or decrease aggregate demand is called demand management.

Time series	In statistics and signal processing, a time series is a sequence of data points, measured typically at successive times, spaced at (often uniform) time intervals. Analysts throughout the economy will use these to aid in the management of their corresponding businesses.
Smoothing	That which involves playing down differences and finding areas of agreement are referred to as accommodation or smoothing.
Analyst	Analyst refers to a person or tool with a primary function of information analysis, generally with a more limited, practical and short term set of goals than a researcher.
Sensitivity analysis	A what-if technique that managers use to examine how a result will change if the original predicted data are not achieved or if an underlying assumption changes is sensitivity analysis.
Sales forecasting	Sales forecasting refers to the process of predicting sales of services or goods. The initial step in preparing a master budget.
Trend	Trend refers to the long-term movement of an economic variable, such as its average rate of increase or decrease over enough years to encompass several business cycles.
Management	Management characterizes the process of leading and directing all or part of an organization, often a business, through the deployment and manipulation of resources. Early twentieth-century management writer Mary Parker Follett defined management as "the art of getting things done through people."
Moving average	A moving average series can be calculated for any time series, but is most often applied to stock prices, returns or trading volumes. Moving averages are used to smooth out short-term fluctuations, thus highlighting longer-term trends or cycles.
Points	Loan origination fees that may be deductible as interest by a buyer of property. A seller of property who pays points reduces the selling price by the amount of the points paid for the buyer.
Weighted average	The weighted average unit cost of the goods available for sale for both cost of goods sold and ending inventory.
Alpha	Alpha is a risk-adjusted measure of the so-called "excess return" on an investment. It is a common measure of assessing active manager's performance as it is the return in excess of a benchmark index or "risk-free" investment.
Seasonal adjustment	The removal of the regular fluctuations in an economic variable that occur as a function of the time of year is referred to as seasonal adjustment.
Heuristic	A heuristic is a particular technique of directing one's attention in learning, discovery, or problem-solving.
Trial	An examination before a competent tribunal, according to the law of the land, of the facts or law put in issue in a cause, for the purpose of determining such issue is a trial. When the court hears and determines any issue of fact or law for the purpose of determining the rights of the parties, it may be considered a trial.

Variable	A variable is something measured by a number; it is used to analyze what happens to other things when the size of that number changes.
Management	Management characterizes the process of leading and directing all or part of an organization, often a business, through the deployment and manipulation of resources. Early twentieth-century management writer Mary Parker Follett defined management as "the art of getting things done through people."
Regression analysis	Regression analysis refers to the statistical technique of finding a straight line that approximates the information in a group of data points. Used throughout empirical economics, including both international trade and finance.
Correlation	A correlation is the measure of the extent to which two economic or statistical variables move together, normalized so that its values range from -1 to +1. It is defined as the covariance of the two variables divided by the square root of the product of their variances.
Assessment	Collecting information and providing feedback to employees about their behavior, communication style, or skills is an assessment.
Perfect information	Perfect information is a term used in economics and game theory to describe a state of complete knowledge about the actions of other players that is instantaneously updated as new information arises.
Sales forecasting	Sales forecasting refers to the process of predicting sales of services or goods. The initial step in preparing a master budget.
Mistake	In contract law a mistake is incorrect understanding by one or more parties to a contract and may be used as grounds to invalidate the agreement. Common law has identified three different types of mistake in contract: unilateral mistake, mutual mistake, and common mistake.
Analyst	Analyst refers to a person or tool with a primary function of information analysis, generally with a more limited, practical and short term set of goals than a researcher.
Future value	Future value measures what money is worth at a specified time in the future assuming a certain interest rate. This is used in time value of money calculations.
Coefficient of determination	A statistic that measures the percentage of variation in a dependent variable explained by one or more independent variables is the coefficient of determination.
Regression line	A line fit to a set of data points using least-squares regression is referred to as a regression line.
Evaluation	The consumer's appraisal of the product or brand on important attributes is called evaluation.
Flowchart	A flowchart is a schematic display of a process. Commonly used to help visualize the content better, or to find flaws in the process.
Context	The effect of the background under which a message often takes on more and richer meaning is a context. Context is especially important in cross-cultural interactions because some cultures are said to be high context or low context.
Industry	A group of firms that produce identical or similar products is an industry. It is also used specifically to refer to an area of economic production focused on manufacturing which involves large amounts of capital investment before any profit can be realized, also called "heavy industry".
Firm	An organization that employs resources to produce a good or service for profit and owns and operates one or more plants is referred to as a firm.
Promotion	Promotion refers to all the techniques sellers use to motivate people to buy products or

services. An attempt by marketers to inform people about products and to persuade them to participate in an exchange.

Sales promotion

Sales promotion refers to the promotional tool that stimulates consumer purchasing and dealer interest by means of short-term activities.

Yield

The interest rate that equates a future value or an annuity to a given present value is a yield.

Consideration

Consideration in contract law, a basic requirement for an enforceable agreement under traditional contract principles, defined in this text as legal value, bargained for and given in exchange for an act or promise. In corporation law, cash or property contributed to a corporation in exchange for shares, or a promise to contribute such cash or property.

Variance

Variance refers to a measure of how much an economic or statistical variable varies across values or observations. Its calculation is the same as that of the covariance, being the covariance of the variable with itself.

Slope

The slope of a line in the plane containing the x and y axes is generally represented by the letter m, and is defined as the change in the y coordinate divided by the corresponding change in the x coordinate, between two distinct points on the line.

Contribution

In business organization law, the cash or property contributed to a business by its owners is referred to as contribution.

Advertising

Advertising refers to paid, nonpersonal communication through various media by organizations and individuals who are in some way identified in the advertising message.

Residual

Residual payments can refer to an ongoing stream of payments in respect of the completion of past achievements.

Inflation

An increase in the overall price level of an economy, usually as measured by the CPI or by the implicit price deflator is called inflation.

Household

An economic unit that provides the economy with resources and uses the income received to purchase goods and services that satisfy economic wants is called household.

Interest

In finance and economics, interest is the price paid by a borrower for the use of a lender's money. In other words, interest is the amount of paid to "rent" money for a period of time.

Interest rate

The rate of return on bonds, loans, or deposits. When one speaks of 'the' interest rate, it is usually in a model where there is only one.

Fixture

Fixture refers to a thing that was originally personal property and that has been actually or constructively affixed to the soil itself or to some structure legally a part of the land.

Production	The creation of finished goods and services using the factors of production: land, labor, capital, entrepreneurship, and knowledge.
Logistics	Those activities that focus on getting the right amount of the right products to the right place at the right time at the lowest possible cost is referred to as logistics.
Management	Management characterizes the process of leading and directing all or part of an organization, often a business, through the deployment and manipulation of resources. Early twentieth-century management writer Mary Parker Follett defined management as "the art of getting things done through people."
Sales forecasting	Sales forecasting refers to the process of predicting sales of services or goods. The initial step in preparing a master budget.
Assessment	Collecting information and providing feedback to employees about their behavior, communication style, or skills is an assessment.
Time series	In statistics and signal processing, a time series is a sequence of data points, measured typically at successive times, spaced at (often uniform) time intervals. Analysts throughout the economy will use these to aid in the management of their corresponding businesses.
Devise	In a will, a gift of real property is called a devise.
Trend	Trend refers to the long-term movement of an economic variable, such as its average rate of increase or decrease over enough years to encompass several business cycles.
Variable	A variable is something measured by a number; it is used to analyze what happens to other things when the size of that number changes.
Marketing	Promoting and selling products or services to customers, or prospective customers, is referred to as marketing.
Channel	Channel, in communications (sometimes called communications channel), refers to the medium used to convey information from a sender (or transmitter) to a receiver.
Analyst	Analyst refers to a person or tool with a primary function of information analysis, generally with a more limited, practical and short term set of goals than a researcher.
Groupthink	Groupthink is a situation in which pressures for cohesion and togetherness are so strong as to produce narrowly considered and bad decisions; this can be especially true via conformity pressures in groups.
Sales forecast	Sales forecast refers to the maximum total sales of a product that a firm expects to sell during a specified time period under specified environmental conditions and its own marketing efforts.
Business plan	A detailed written statement that describes the nature of the business, the target market, the advantages the business will have in relation to competition, and the resources and qualifications of the owner is referred to as a business plan.
Committee	A long-lasting, sometimes permanent team in the organization structure created to deal with tasks that recur regularly is the committee.
Evaluation	The consumer's appraisal of the product or brand on important attributes is called evaluation.
Revenue	Revenue is a U.S. business term for the amount of money that a company receives from its activities, mostly from sales of products and/or services to customers.
Quota	A government-imposed restriction on quantity, or sometimes on total value, used to restrict the import of something to a specific quantity is called a quota.

Inventory	Tangible property held for sale in the normal course of business or used in producing goods or services for sale is an inventory.
Promotion	Promotion refers to all the techniques sellers use to motivate people to buy products or services. An attempt by marketers to inform people about products and to persuade them to participate in an exchange.
Stock	In financial terminology, stock is the capital raized by a corporation, through the issuance and sale of shares.
Points	Loan origination fees that may be deductible as interest by a buyer of property. A seller of property who pays points reduces the selling price by the amount of the points paid for the buyer.
Correlation	A correlation is the measure of the extent to which two economic or statistical variables move together, normalized so that its values range from -1 to +1. It is defined as the covariance of the two variables divided by the square root of the product of their variances.
Context	The effect of the background under which a message often takes on more and richer meaning is a context. Context is especially important in cross-cultural interactions because some cultures are said to be high context or low context.
Jury	A body of lay persons, selected by lot, or by some other fair and impartial means, to ascertain, under the guidance of the judge, the truth in questions of fact arising either in civil litigation or a criminal process is referred to as jury.
Delphi method	The Delphi method has traditionally been a technique aimed at building an agreement, or consensus about an opinion or view, without necessarily having people meet face to face, such as through surveys, questionnaires, emails etc.
Market	A market is, as defined in economics, a social arrangement that allows buyers and sellers to discover information and carry out a voluntary exchange of goods or services.
Market research	Market research is the process of systematic gathering, recording and analyzing of data about customers, competitors and the market. Market research can help create a business plan, launch a new product or service, fine tune existing products and services, expand into new markets etc. It can be used to determine which portion of the population will purchase the product/service, based on variables like age, gender, location and income level. It can be found out what market characteristics your target market has.
Product line	A group of products that are physically similar or are intended for a similar market are called the product line.
Contribution	In business organization law, the cash or property contributed to a business by its owners is referred to as contribution.
Industry	A group of firms that produce identical or similar products is an industry. It is also used specifically to refer to an area of economic production focused on manufacturing which involves large amounts of capital investment before any profit can be realized, also called "heavy industry".
Personnel	A collective term for all of the employees of an organization. Personnel is also commonly used to refer to the personnel management function or the organizational unit responsible for administering personnel programs.
Consultant	A professional that provides expert advice in a particular field or area in which customers occassionaly require this type of knowledge is a consultant.
Operation	A standardized method or technique that is performed repetitively, often on different materials resulting in different finished goods is called an operation.

Go to **Cram101.com** for the Practice Tests for this Chapter.

Post hoc	Post hoc refers to literally, 'after this, therefore because of this."
Sales management	Planning the selling program and implementing and controlling the personal selling effort of the firm is called sales management.
Gap	In December of 1995, Gap became the first major North American retailer to accept independent monitoring of the working conditions in a contract factory producing its garments. Gap is the largest specialty retailer in the United States.
Supply chain	Supply chain refers to the flow of goods, services, and information from the initial sources of materials and services to the delivery of products to consumers.
Interest	In finance and economics, interest is the price paid by a borrower for the use of a lender's money. In other words, interest is the amount of paid to "rent" money for a period of time.
Supply	Supply is the aggregate amount of any material good that can be called into being at a certain price point; it comprises one half of the equation of supply and demand. In classical economic theory, a curve representing supply is one of the factors that produce price.
Service	Service refers to a "non tangible product" that is not embodied in a physical good and that typically effects some change in another product, person, or institution. Contrasts with good.
Assignment	A transfer of property or some right or interest is referred to as assignment.
Adjuster	A person who settles insurance claims by calculating the amount of loss or damage is an adjuster. This person may work for the insurance company or an independent adjusting company.
Portfolio	In finance, a portfolio is a collection of investments held by an institution or a private individual. Holding but not always a portfolio is part of an investment and risk-limiting strategy called diversification. By owning several assets, certain types of risk (in particular specific risk) can be reduced.
Bottom line	The bottom line is net income on the last line of a income statement.
Audit	An examination of the financial reports to ensure that they represent what they claim and conform with generally accepted accounting principles is referred to as audit.
Supply chain management	Supply chain management deals with the planning and execution issues involved in managing a supply chain. Supply chain management spans all movement and storage of raw materials, work-in-process inventory, and finished goods from point-of-origin to point-of-consumption.
Vendor	A person who sells property to a vendee is a vendor. The words vendor and vendee are more commonly applied to the seller and purchaser of real estate, and the words seller and buyer are more commonly applied to the seller and purchaser of personal property.
Strategic alliance	Strategic alliance refers to a long-term partnership between two or more companies established to help each company build competitive market advantages.
Collaboration	Collaboration occurs when the interaction between groups is very important to goal attainment and the goals are compatible. Wherein people work together —applying both to the work of individuals as well as larger collectives and societies.
Liability	A liability is a present obligation of the enterprise arizing from past events, the settlement of which is expected to result in an outflow from the enterprise of resources embodying economic benefits.
Product concept	The verbal and perhaps pictorial description of the benefits and features of a proposed product; also the early stage of the product development process in which only the product concept exists.
Shares	Shares refer to an equity security, representing a shareholder's ownership of a corporation.

Go to **Cram101.com** for the Practice Tests for this Chapter.

	Shares are one of a finite number of equal portions in the capital of a company, entitling the owner to a proportion of distributed, non-reinvested profits known as dividends and to a portion of the value of the company in case of liquidation.
Extension	Extension refers to an out-of-court settlement in which creditors agree to allow the firm more time to meet its financial obligations. A new repayment schedule will be developed, subject to the acceptance of creditors.
Marketing research	Marketing research refers to the analysis of markets to determine opportunities and challenges, and to find the information needed to make good decisions.
Primary data	Facts and figures that are newly collected for the project are referred to as primary data.
Focus group	A small group of people who meet under the direction of a discussion leader to communicate their opinions about an organization, its products, or other given issues is a focus group.
Household	An economic unit that provides the economy with resources and uses the income received to purchase goods and services that satisfy economic wants is called household.
Exchange	The trade of things of value between buyer and seller so that each is better off after the trade is called the exchange.
Adoption	In corporation law, a corporation's acceptance of a pre-incorporation contract by action of its board of directors, by which the corporation becomes liable on the contract, is referred to as adoption.
Users	Users refer to people in the organization who actually use the product or service purchased by the buying center.
Consideration	Consideration in contract law, a basic requirement for an enforceable agreement under traditional contract principles, defined in this text as legal value, bargained for and given in exchange for an act or promise. In corporation law, cash or property contributed to a corporation in exchange for shares, or a promise to contribute such cash or property.
Economics	The social science dealing with the use of scarce resources to obtain the maximum satisfaction of society's virtually unlimited economic wants is an economics.
Security	Security refers to a claim on the borrower future income that is sold by the borrower to the lender. A security is a type of transferable interest representing financial value.
Securities and exchange commission	Securities and exchange commission refers to U.S. government agency that determines the financial statements that public companies must provide to stockholders and the measurement rules that they must use in producing those statements.
Commerce	Commerce is the exchange of something of value between two entities. It is the central mechanism from which capitalism is derived.
Economy	The income, expenditures, and resources that affect the cost of running a business and household are called an economy.
Business cycle	Business cycle refers to the pattern followed by macroeconommic variables, such as GDP and unemployment that rise and fall irregularly over time, relative to trend.
Business analysis	Business analysis is a structured methodology that is focused on completely understanding the customer's needs, identifying how best to meet those needs, and then "reinventing" the stream of processes to meet those needs.
Durable good	A durable good is a good which does not quickly wear out, or more specifically, it yields services or utility over time rather than being completely used up when used once.
Money supply	There are several formal definitions, but all include the quantity of currency in circulation plus the amount of demand deposits. The money supply, together with the amount of real

Go to **Cram101.com** for the Practice Tests for this Chapter.

economic activity in a country, is an important determinant of price.

Competitor	Other organizations in the same industry or type of business that provide a good or service to the same set of customers is referred to as a competitor.
Elasticity	In economics, elasticity is the ratio of the incremental percentage change in one variable with respect to an incremental percentage change in another variable. Elasticity is usually expressed as a positive number (i.e., an absolute value) when the sign is already clear from context.
Contract	A contract is a "promise" or an "agreement" that is enforced or recognized by the law. In the civil law, a contract is considered to be part of the general law of obligations.
Capital	Capital generally refers to financial wealth, especially that used to start or maintain a business. In classical economics, capital is one of four factors of production, the others being land and labor and entrepreneurship.
Profit	Profit refers to the return to the resource entrepreneurial ability; total revenue minus total cost.
Bond	Bond refers to a debt instrument, issued by a borrower and promising a specified stream of payments to the purchaser, usually regular interest payments plus a final repayment of principal.
Price elasticity of demand	Price elasticity of demand refers to the ratio of the percentage change in quantity demanded of a product or resource to the percentage change in its price; a measure of the responsiveness of buyers to a change in the price of a product or resource.
Leading indicator	A leading indicator is an economic indicator, such as stock prices and average work hours in a manufacturing sector, which tend to change before the general economic activity.
Price elasticity	The responsiveness of the market to change in price is called price elasticity. If price elasticity is low, a large change in price will lead to a small change in supply.
Manufacturing	Production of goods primarily by the application of labor and capital to raw materials and other intermediate inputs, in contrast to agriculture, mining, forestry, fishing, and services a manufacturing.
Appropriation	A privacy tort that consists of using a person's name or likeness for commercial gain without the person's permission is an appropriation.
Advertising	Advertising refers to paid, nonpersonal communication through various media by organizations and individuals who are in some way identified in the advertising message.
Market share	That fraction of an industry's output accounted for by an individual firm or group of firms is called market share.
Decision tree	In decision theory, a decision tree is a graph of decisions and their possible consequences, (including resource costs and risks) used to create a plan to reach a goal.
Enabling	Enabling refers to giving workers the education and tools they need to assume their new decision-making powers.
Retail sale	The sale of goods and services to consumers for their own use is a retail sale.
Respondent	Respondent refers to a term often used to describe the party charged in an administrative proceeding. The party adverse to the appellant in a case appealed to a higher court.
Demographic	A demographic is a term used in marketing and broadcasting, to describe a demographic grouping or a market segment.
Consumer good	Products and services that are ultimately consumed rather than used in the production of

Go to **Cram101.com** for the Practice Tests for this Chapter.

	another good are a consumer good.
Distribution	Distribution in economics, the manner in which total output and income is distributed among individuals or factors.
Firm	An organization that employs resources to produce a good or service for profit and owns and operates one or more plants is referred to as a firm.

Management	Management characterizes the process of leading and directing all or part of an organization, often a business, through the deployment and manipulation of resources. Early twentieth-century management writer Mary Parker Follett defined management as "the art of getting things done through people."
Management information system	A computer-based system that provides information and support for effective managerial decision makin is referred to as a management information system.
Information system	An information system is a system whether automated or manual, that comprises people, machines, and/or methods organized to collect, process, transmit, and disseminate data that represent user information.
Users	Users refer to people in the organization who actually use the product or service purchased by the buying center.
Sales forecast	Sales forecast refers to the maximum total sales of a product that a firm expects to sell during a specified time period under specified environmental conditions and its own marketing efforts.
Sales forecasting	Sales forecasting refers to the process of predicting sales of services or goods. The initial step in preparing a master budget.
Time series	In statistics and signal processing, a time series is a sequence of data points, measured typically at successive times, spaced at (often uniform) time intervals. Analysts throughout the economy will use these to aid in the management of their corresponding businesses.
Inventory	Tangible property held for sale in the normal course of business or used in producing goods or services for sale is an inventory.
Confirmed	When the seller's bank agrees to assume liability on the letter of credit issued by the buyer's bank the transaction is confirmed. The term means that the credit is not only backed up by the issuing foreign bank, but that payment is also guaranteed by the notifying American bank.
Market	A market is, as defined in economics, a social arrangement that allows buyers and sellers to discover information and carry out a voluntary exchange of goods or services.
Market research	Market research is the process of systematic gathering, recording and analyzing of data about customers, competitors and the market. Market research can help create a business plan, launch a new product or service, fine tune existing products and services, expand into new markets etc. It can be used to determine which portion of the population will purchase the product/service, based on variables like age, gender, location and income level. It can be found out what market characteristics your target market has.
Mistake	In contract law a mistake is incorrect understanding by one or more parties to a contract and may be used as grounds to invalidate the agreement. Common law has identified three different types of mistake in contract: unilateral mistake, mutual mistake, and common mistake.
Creep	Creep is a problem in project management where the initial objectives of the project are jeopardized by a gradual increase in overall objectives as the project progresses.
Functional manager	A manager who is responsible for a department that performs a single functional task and has employees with similar training and skills is referred to as a functional manager.
Warehouse	Warehouse refers to a location, often decentralized, that a firm uses to store, consolidate, age, or mix stock; house product-recall programs; or ease tax burdens.
Data warehouse	A Data warehouse is a repository of integrated information, available for queries and analysis. Data and information are extracted from heterogeneous sources as they are

Go to **Cram101.com** for the Practice Tests for this Chapter.

generated.

Open system	A system that interacts with its environment is referred to as open system. It is a system that takes in (raw materials, capital, skilled labor) and converts them into goods and services (via machinery, human skills) that are sent back to that environment, where they are bought by customers.
Production	The creation of finished goods and services using the factors of production: land, labor, capital, entrepreneurship, and knowledge.
Regression analysis	Regression analysis refers to the statistical technique of finding a straight line that approximates the information in a group of data points. Used throughout empirical economics, including both international trade and finance.
Financial plan	The financial plan section of a business plan consists of three financial statements (the income statement, the cash flow projection, and the balance sheet) and a brief analysis of these three statements.
Vendor	A person who sells property to a vendee is a vendor. The words vendor and vendee are more commonly applied to the seller and purchaser of real estate, and the words seller and buyer are more commonly applied to the seller and purchaser of personal property.
Marketing	Promoting and selling products or services to customers, or prospective customers, is referred to as marketing.
Financial analysis	Financial analysis is the analysis of the accounts and the economic prospects of a firm.
Marketing research	Marketing research refers to the analysis of markets to determine opportunities and challenges, and to find the information needed to make good decisions.
Management system	A management system is the framework of processes and procedures used to ensure that an organization can fulfill all tasks required to achieve its objectives.
Product line	A group of products that are physically similar or are intended for a similar market are called the product line.
Stock	In financial terminology, stock is the capital raized by a corporation, through the issuance and sale of shares.
Stock keeping unit	Stock keeping unit refers to a unique identification number that defines an item for ordering or inventory purposes.
Corporate level	Corporate level refers to level at which top management directs overall strategy for the entire organization.
Analyst	Analyst refers to a person or tool with a primary function of information analysis, generally with a more limited, practical and short term set of goals than a researcher.
Technology	The body of knowledge and techniques that can be used to combine economic resources to produce goods and services is called technology.
Trend	Trend refers to the long-term movement of an economic variable, such as its average rate of increase or decrease over enough years to encompass several business cycles.
Promotion	Promotion refers to all the techniques sellers use to motivate people to buy products or services. An attempt by marketers to inform people about products and to persuade them to participate in an exchange.
Correlation	A correlation is the measure of the extent to which two economic or statistical variables move together, normalized so that its values range from -1 to +1. It is defined as the covariance of the two variables divided by the square root of the product of their variances.

Expert system	Computer systems incorporating the decision rules of people recognized as experts in a certain area are refered to as an expert system.
Variable	A variable is something measured by a number; it is used to analyze what happens to other things when the size of that number changes.
Trust	An arrangement in which shareholders of independent firms agree to give up their stock in exchange for trust certificates that entitle them to a share of the trust's common profits.
Management by exception	A tool used by a marketing manager that involves identifying results that deviate from plans, diagnosing their cause, making appropriate new plans, and taking new actions is called management by exception.
Supply chain	Supply chain refers to the flow of goods, services, and information from the initial sources of materials and services to the delivery of products to consumers.
Service	Service refers to a "non tangible product" that is not embodied in a physical good and that typically effects some change in another product, person, or institution. Contrasts with good.
Supply	Supply is the aggregate amount of any material good that can be called into being at a certain price point; it comprises one half of the equation of supply and demand. In classical economic theory, a curve representing supply is one of the factors that produce price.
Customer service	The ability of logistics management to satisfy users in terms of time, dependability, communication, and convenience is called the customer service.
Smoothing	That which involves playing down differences and finding areas of agreement are referred to as accommodation or smoothing.
Residual	Residual payments can refer to an ongoing stream of payments in respect of the completion of past achievements.
Exogenous variable	Exogenous variable refers to a variable that is taken as given by an economic model. It therefore is subject to direct manipulation by the modeler. In most models, policy variables such as tariffs and par values of pegged exchange rates are exogenous.
Distribution	Distribution in economics, the manner in which total output and income is distributed among individuals or factors.
Conversion	Conversion refers to any distinct act of dominion wrongfully exerted over another's personal property in denial of or inconsistent with his rights therein. That tort committed by a person who deals with chattels not belonging to him in a manner that is inconsistent with the ownership of the lawful owner.
Hierarchy	A system of grouping people in an organization according to rank from the top down in which all subordinate managers must report to one person is called a hierarchy.
Distribution center	Designed to facilitate the timely movement of goods and represent a very important part of a supply chain is a distribution center.
Option	A contract that gives the purchaser the option to buy or sell the underlying financial instrument at a specified price, called the exercise price or strike price, within a specific period of time.
Future value	Future value measures what money is worth at a specified time in the future assuming a certain interest rate. This is used in time value of money calculations.
Default	In finance, default occurs when a debtor has not met its legal obligations according to the debt contract, e.g. it has not made a scheduled payment, or violated a covenant (condition) of the debt contract.

Total demand	Total demand refers to the demand schedule or the demand curve of all buyers of a good or service; also called market demand.
Export	In economics, an export is any good or commodity, shipped or otherwise transported out of a country, province, town to another part of the world in a legitimate fashion, typically for use in trade or sale.
Assessment	Collecting information and providing feedback to employees about their behavior, communication style, or skills is an assessment.
Peak	Peak refers to the point in the business cycle when an economic expansion reaches its highest point before turning down. Contrasts with trough.
Trough	Trough refers to the point in the business cycle when an economic contraction reaches its lowest point before turning up.
Standard deviation	A measure of the spread or dispersion of a series of numbers around the expected value is the standard deviation. The standard deviation tells us how well the expected value represents a series of values.
Slope	The slope of a line in the plane containing the x and y axes is generally represented by the letter m, and is defined as the change in the y coordinate divided by the corresponding change in the x coordinate, between two distinct points on the line.
Converse	Converse is an American shoe company which has been making shoes since the early 20th century. The company's main turning point came in 1917 when the Converse All-Star basketball shoe was introduced. This was a real innovation at the time, considering the sport was only 25 years old.

Benchmarking	The continuous process of comparing the levels of performance in producing products and services and executing activities against the best levels of performance is benchmarking.
Sales forecasting	Sales forecasting refers to the process of predicting sales of services or goods. The initial step in preparing a master budget.
Management	Management characterizes the process of leading and directing all or part of an organization, often a business, through the deployment and manipulation of resources. Early twentieth-century management writer Mary Parker Follett defined management as "the art of getting things done through people."
Interest	In finance and economics, interest is the price paid by a borrower for the use of a lender's money. In other words, interest is the amount of paid to "rent" money for a period of time.
Demographic	A demographic is a term used in marketing and broadcasting, to describe a demographic grouping or a market segment.
Respondent	Respondent refers to a term often used to describe the party charged in an administrative proceeding. The party adverse to the appellant in a case appealed to a higher court.
Firm	An organization that employs resources to produce a good or service for profit and owns and operates one or more plants is referred to as a firm.
Asset	An item of property, such as land, capital, money, a share in ownership, or a claim on others for future payment, such as a bond or a bank deposit is an asset.
Smoothing	That which involves playing down differences and finding areas of agreement are referred to as accommodation or smoothing.
Jury	A body of lay persons, selected by lot, or by some other fair and impartial means, to ascertain, under the guidance of the judge, the truth in questions of fact arising either in civil litigation or a criminal process is referred to as jury.
Moving average	A moving average series can be calculated for any time series, but is most often applied to stock prices, returns or trading volumes. Moving averages are used to smooth out short-term fluctuations, thus highlighting longer-term trends or cycles.
Time series	In statistics and signal processing, a time series is a sequence of data points, measured typically at successive times, spaced at (often uniform) time intervals. Analysts throughout the economy will use these to aid in the management of their corresponding businesses.
Time horizon	A time horizon is a fixed point of time in the future at which point certain processes will be evaluated or assumed to end. It is necessary in an accounting, finance or risk management regime to assign such a fixed horizon time so that alternatives can be evaluated for performance over the same period of time.
Trend	Trend refers to the long-term movement of an economic variable, such as its average rate of increase or decrease over enough years to encompass several business cycles.
Integration	Economic integration refers to reducing barriers among countries to transactions and to movements of goods, capital, and labor, including harmonization of laws, regulations, and standards. Integrated markets theoretically function as a unified market.
Production	The creation of finished goods and services using the factors of production: land, labor, capital, entrepreneurship, and knowledge.
Inventory	Tangible property held for sale in the normal course of business or used in producing goods or services for sale is an inventory.
Logistics	Those activities that focus on getting the right amount of the right products to the right place at the right time at the lowest possible cost is referred to as logistics.

Marketing	Promoting and selling products or services to customers, or prospective customers, is referred to as marketing.
Management information system	A computer-based system that provides information and support for effective managerial decision makin is referred to as a management information system.
Information system	An information system is a system whether automated or manual, that comprises people, machines, and/or methods organized to collect, process, transmit, and disseminate data that represent user information.
Sales forecast	Sales forecast refers to the maximum total sales of a product that a firm expects to sell during a specified time period under specified environmental conditions and its own marketing efforts.
Market	A market is, as defined in economics, a social arrangement that allows buyers and sellers to discover information and carry out a voluntary exchange of goods or services.
Market research	Market research is the process of systematic gathering, recording and analyzing of data about customers, competitors and the market. Market research can help create a business plan, launch a new product or service, fine tune existing products and services, expand into new markets etc. It can be used to determine which portion of the population will purchase the product/service, based on variables like age, gender, location and income level. It can be found out what market characteristics your target market has.
Supply chain	Supply chain refers to the flow of goods, services, and information from the initial sources of materials and services to the delivery of products to consumers.
Innovation	Innovation refers to the first commercially successful introduction of a new product, the use of a new method of production, or the creation of a new form of business organization.
Supply	Supply is the aggregate amount of any material good that can be called into being at a certain price point; it comprises one half of the equation of supply and demand. In classical economic theory, a curve representing supply is one of the factors that produce price.
Electronic data interchange	Electronic data interchange refers to the direct exchange between organizations of data via a computer-to-computer interface.
Channel	Channel, in communications (sometimes called communications channel), refers to the medium used to convey information from a sender (or transmitter) to a receiver.
Product line	A group of products that are physically similar or are intended for a similar market are called the product line.
Stock	In financial terminology, stock is the capital raized by a corporation, through the issuance and sale of shares.
Stock keeping unit	Stock keeping unit refers to a unique identification number that defines an item for ordering or inventory purposes.
Personnel	A collective term for all of the employees of an organization. Personnel is also commonly used to refer to the personnel management function or the organizational unit responsible for administering personnel programs.
Business plan	A detailed written statement that describes the nature of the business, the target market, the advantages the business will have in relation to competition, and the resources and qualifications of the owner is referred to as a business plan.
Budget	Budget refers to an account, usually for a year, of the planned expenditures and the expected receipts of an entity. For a government, the receipts are tax revenues.

Performance measurement	The process by which someone evaluates an employee's work behaviors by measurement and comparison with previously established standards, documents the results, and communicates the results to the employee is called performance measurement.
Buyer	A buyer refers to a role in the buying center with formal authority and responsibility to select the supplier and negotiate the terms of the contract.
Consumer market	All the individuals or households that want goods and services for personal consumption or use are a consumer market.
Elasticity	In economics, elasticity is the ratio of the incremental percentage change in one variable with respect to an incremental percentage change in another variable. Elasticity is usually expressed as a positive number (i.e., an absolute value) when the sign is already clear from context.
Short run	Short run refers to a period of time that permits an increase or decrease in current production volume with existing capacity, but one that is too short to permit enlargement of that capacity itself (eg, the building of new plants, training of additional workers, etc.).
Inelastic	Inelastic refers to having an elasticity less than one. For a price elasticity of demand, this means that expenditure falls as price falls. For an income elasticity, it means that expenditure share falls with income.
Inelastic demand	Inelastic demand refers to product or resource demand for which the elasticity coefficient for price is less than 1. This means the resulting percentage change in quantity demanded is less than the percentage change in price. In other words, consumers are relatively less sensitive to changes in price.
Market structure	Market structure refers to the way that suppliers and demanders in an industry interact to determine price and quantity. Market structures range from perfect competition to monopoly.
Advertising	Advertising refers to paid, nonpersonal communication through various media by organizations and individuals who are in some way identified in the advertising message.
Operation	A standardized method or technique that is performed repetitively, often on different materials resulting in different finished goods is called an operation.
Contract	A contract is a "promise" or an "agreement" that is enforced or recognized by the law. In the civil law, a contract is considered to be part of the general law of obligations.
Discount	The difference between the face value of a bond and its selling price, when a bond is sold for less than its face value it's referred to as a discount.
Quantity discounts	Quantity discounts refer to reductions in unit costs for a larger order.
Quantity discount	A quantity discount is a price reduction given for a large order.
Preference	The act of a debtor in paying or securing one or more of his creditors in a manner more favorable to them than to other creditors or to the exclusion of such other creditors is a preference. In the absence of statute, a preference is perfectly good, but to be legal it must be bona fide, and not a mere subterfuge of the debtor to secure a future benefit to himself or to prevent the application of his property to his debts.
Leading indicator	A leading indicator is an economic indicator, such as stock prices and average work hours in a manufacturing sector, which tend to change before the general economic activity.
Econometric model	A model whose equations are estimated using statistical procedures is an econometric model. They are used by economists to find standard relationships among aspects of the macroeconomy and use those relationships to predict the effects of certain events (like government

policies) on inflation, unemployment, growth, etc...

Distribution	Distribution in economics, the manner in which total output and income is distributed among individuals or factors.
Technology	The body of knowledge and techniques that can be used to combine economic resources to produce goods and services is called technology.
Materials requirement planning	A computer-based production management system that uses sales forecasts to make sure that needed parts and materials are available at the right time and place is referred to as materials requirement planning.
Volatility	Volatility refers to the extent to which an economic variable, such as a price or an exchange rate, moves up and down over time.
Premium	Premium refers to the fee charged by an insurance company for an insurance policy. The rate of losses must be relatively predictable: In order to set the premium (prices) insurers must be able to estimate them accurately.
Information technology	Information technology refers to technology that helps companies change business by allowing them to use new methods.
Regression analysis	Regression analysis refers to the statistical technique of finding a straight line that approximates the information in a group of data points. Used throughout empirical economics, including both international trade and finance.
Consumer behavior	Consumer behavior refers to the actions a person takes in purchasing and using products and services, including the mental and social processes that precede and follow these actions.
Variable	A variable is something measured by a number; it is used to analyze what happens to other things when the size of that number changes.
Neural network	A neural network is a non-linear statistical data modeling tool. They can be used to model complex relationships between inputs and outputs or to find patterns in data.
Corporate level	Corporate level refers to level at which top management directs overall strategy for the entire organization.
Weighted average	The weighted average unit cost of the goods available for sale for both cost of goods sold and ending inventory.
Warrant	A warrant is a security that entitles the holder to buy or sell a certain additional quantity of an underlying security at an agreed-upon price, at the holder's discretion.
Evaluation	The consumer's appraisal of the product or brand on important attributes is called evaluation.
Continuous improvement	The constant effort to eliminate waste, reduce response time, simplify the design of both products and processes, and improve quality and customer service is referred to as continuous improvement.
Financial plan	The financial plan section of a business plan consists of three financial statements (the income statement, the cash flow projection, and the balance sheet) and a brief analysis of these three statements.
Distribution channel	A distribution channel is a chain of intermediaries, each passing a product down the chain to the next organization, before it finally reaches the consumer or end-user.
Vendor	A person who sells property to a vendee is a vendor. The words vendor and vendee are more commonly applied to the seller and purchaser of real estate, and the words seller and buyer are more commonly applied to the seller and purchaser of personal property.

Anticipation	In finance, anticipation is where debts are paid off early, generally in order to pay less interest.
Best practice	Best practice is a management idea which asserts that there is a technique, method, process, activity, incentive or reward that is more effective at delivering a particular outcome than any other technique, method, process, etc.

Management	Management characterizes the process of leading and directing all or part of an organization, often a business, through the deployment and manipulation of resources. Early twentieth-century management writer Mary Parker Follett defined management as "the art of getting things done through people."
Sales forecasting	Sales forecasting refers to the process of predicting sales of services or goods. The initial step in preparing a master budget.
Supply chain	Supply chain refers to the flow of goods, services, and information from the initial sources of materials and services to the delivery of products to consumers.
Supply	Supply is the aggregate amount of any material good that can be called into being at a certain price point; it comprises one half of the equation of supply and demand. In classical economic theory, a curve representing supply is one of the factors that produce price.
Distribution	Distribution in economics, the manner in which total output and income is distributed among individuals or factors.
Pillsbury	Pillsbury the company was the first in the United States to use steam rollers for processing grain. The finished product required transportation, so the Pillsburys assisted in funding railroad development in Minnesota.
Coca Cola	As a publicity marketing strategy started by Ernest Woodruff, the company presents the formula of Coca Cola as one of the most closely held trade secrets in modern business that only a few employees know or have access to.
Nabisco	In 2000 Philip Morris Companies acquired Nabisco; that acquisition was approved by the Federal Trade Commission subject to the divestiture of products in five areas: three Jell-O and Royal brands types of products (dry-mix gelatin dessert, dry-mix pudding, no-bake desserts), intense mints (such as Altoids), and baking powder. Kraft later purchased the company.
Firm	An organization that employs resources to produce a good or service for profit and owns and operates one or more plants is referred to as a firm.
Federal Express	The company officially began operations on April 17, 1973, utilizing a network of 14 Dassault Falcon 20s which connected 25 U.S. cities. FedEx, the first cargo airline to use jet aircraft for its services, expanded greatly after the deregulation of the cargo airlines sector. Federal Express use of the hub-spoke distribution paradigm in air freight enabled it to become a world leader in its field.
Users	Users refer to people in the organization who actually use the product or service purchased by the buying center.
Sales forecast	Sales forecast refers to the maximum total sales of a product that a firm expects to sell during a specified time period under specified environmental conditions and its own marketing efforts.
Transcript	A copy of writing is referred to as a transcript. It is the official record of proceedings in a trial or hearing.
Technology	The body of knowledge and techniques that can be used to combine economic resources to produce goods and services is called technology.
Michelin	Incorporated on May 28, 1888, Michelin's activities date back to 1830 in vulcanized rubber, before they moved into tires for bicycles and later for cars. Michelin owned the automobile manufacturer Citroën between 1934 and 1976.
Motorola	The Six Sigma quality system was developed at Motorola even though it became most well known because of its use by General Electric. It was created by engineer Bill Smith, under the

	direction of Bob Galvin (son of founder Paul Galvin) when he was running the company.
DuPont	DuPont was the inventor of CFCs (along with General Motors) and the largest producer of these ozone depleting chemicals (used primarily in aerosol sprays and refrigerants) in the world, with a 25% market share in the late 1980s.
Union	A worker association that bargains with employers over wages and working conditions is called a union.
Exxon	Exxon formally replaced the Esso, Enco, and Humble brands on January 1, 1973, in the USA. The name Esso, pronounced S-O, attracted protests from other Standard Oil spinoffs because of its similarity to the name of the parent company, Standard Oil.
Lucent Technologies	Lucent Technologies is a company composed of what was formerly AT&T Technologies, which included Western Electric and Bell Labs. It was spun-off from AT&T on September 30, 1996. On April 2, 2006, they announced a merger with its French competitor, Alcatel. The combined company has revenues of approximately $25 billion U.S. based on 2005 calendar results.
Integration	Economic integration refers to reducing barriers among countries to transactions and to movements of goods, capital, and labor, including harmonization of laws, regulations, and standards. Integrated markets theoretically function as a unified market.
Purchasing	Purchasing refers to the function in a firm that searches for quality material resources, finds the best suppliers, and negotiates the best price for goods and services.
Production	The creation of finished goods and services using the factors of production: land, labor, capital, entrepreneurship, and knowledge.
Logistics	Those activities that focus on getting the right amount of the right products to the right place at the right time at the lowest possible cost is referred to as logistics.
Marketing	Promoting and selling products or services to customers, or prospective customers, is referred to as marketing.
Collaboration	Collaboration occurs when the interaction between groups is very important to goal attainment and the goals are compatible. Wherein people work together —applying both to the work of individuals as well as larger collectives and societies.
Operation	A standardized method or technique that is performed repetitively, often on different materials resulting in different finished goods is called an operation.
Contribution	In business organization law, the cash or property contributed to a business by its owners is referred to as contribution.
Personnel	A collective term for all of the employees of an organization. Personnel is also commonly used to refer to the personnel management function or the organizational unit responsible for administering personnel programs.
Effective communication	When the intended meaning equals the perceived meaning it is called effective communication.
Context	The effect of the background under which a message often takes on more and richer meaning is a context. Context is especially important in cross-cultural interactions because some cultures are said to be high context or low context.
Time horizon	A time horizon is a fixed point of time in the future at which point certain processes will be evaluated or assumed to end. It is necessary in an accounting, finance or risk management regime to assign such a fixed horizon time so that alternatives can be evaluated for performance over the same period of time.
Gap	In December of 1995, Gap became the first major North American retailer to accept independent

monitoring of the working conditions in a contract factory producing its garments. Gap is the largest specialty retailer in the United States.

Organizational culture	The mindset of employees, including their shared beliefs, values, and goals is called the organizational culture.
Approach stage	In the personal selling process, the initial meeting between the salesperson and prospect, where the objectives are to gain the prospect's attention, stimulate interest, and build the foundation for the sales presentation itself and the basis for a working relationship is the approach stage.
Best efforts	Best efforts refer to a distribution in which the investment banker agrees to work for a commission rather than actually underwriting the issue for resale. It is a procedure that is used by smaller investment bankers with relatively unknown companies. The investment banker is not directly taking the risk for distribution.
Product mix	The combination of product lines offered by a manufacturer is referred to as product mix.
Product life cycle	Product life cycle refers to a series of phases in a product's sales and cash flows over time; these phases, in order of occurrence, are introductory, growth, maturity, and decline.
Portfolio	In finance, a portfolio is a collection of investments held by an institution or a private individual. Holding but not always a portfolio is part of an investment and risk-limiting strategy called diversification. By owning several assets, certain types of risk (in particular specific risk) can be reduced.
Hierarchy	A system of grouping people in an organization according to rank from the top down in which all subordinate managers must report to one person is called a hierarchy.
Business plan	A detailed written statement that describes the nature of the business, the target market, the advantages the business will have in relation to competition, and the resources and qualifications of the owner is referred to as a business plan.
Market share	That fraction of an industry's output accounted for by an individual firm or group of firms is called market share.
Industry	A group of firms that produce identical or similar products is an industry. It is also used specifically to refer to an area of economic production focused on manufacturing which involves large amounts of capital investment before any profit can be realized, also called "heavy industry".
Market	A market is, as defined in economics, a social arrangement that allows buyers and sellers to discover information and carry out a voluntary exchange of goods or services.
Accounting	A system that collects and processes financial information about an organization and reports that information to decision makers is referred to as accounting.
Channel	Channel, in communications (sometimes called communications channel), refers to the medium used to convey information from a sender (or transmitter) to a receiver.
Point of Sale	Point of sale can mean a retail shop, a checkout counter in a shop, or a variable location where a transaction occurs.
Inventory	Tangible property held for sale in the normal course of business or used in producing goods or services for sale is an inventory.
Enabling	Enabling refers to giving workers the education and tools they need to assume their new decision-making powers.
Manufacturing	Production of goods primarily by the application of labor and capital to raw materials and other intermediate inputs, in contrast to agriculture, mining, forestry, fishing, and

services a manufacturing.

Assessment	Collecting information and providing feedback to employees about their behavior, communication style, or skills is an assessment.
Devise	In a will, a gift of real property is called a devise.
Vendor	A person who sells property to a vendee is a vendor. The words vendor and vendee are more commonly applied to the seller and purchaser of real estate, and the words seller and buyer are more commonly applied to the seller and purchaser of personal property.
Promotion	Promotion refers to all the techniques sellers use to motivate people to buy products or services. An attempt by marketers to inform people about products and to persuade them to participate in an exchange.
Shelf life	Shelf life is the length of time that corresponds to a tolerable loss in quality of a processed food and other perishable items.
Service	Service refers to a "non tangible product" that is not embodied in a physical good and that typically effects some change in another product, person, or institution. Contrasts with good.
Customer service	The ability of logistics management to satisfy users in terms of time, dependability, communication, and convenience is called the customer service.
Raw material	Raw material refers to a good that has not been transformed by production; a primary product.
Appreciation	Appreciation refers to a rise in the value of a country's currency on the exchange market, relative either to a particular other currency or to a weighted average of other currencies. The currency is said to appreciate. Opposite of 'depreciation.' Appreciation can also refer to the increase in value of any asset.
Points	Loan origination fees that may be deductible as interest by a buyer of property. A seller of property who pays points reduces the selling price by the amount of the points paid for the buyer.
Time series	In statistics and signal processing, a time series is a sequence of data points, measured typically at successive times, spaced at (often uniform) time intervals. Analysts throughout the economy will use these to aid in the management of their corresponding businesses.
Investment	Investment refers to spending for the production and accumulation of capital and additions to inventories. In a financial sense, buying an asset with the expectation of making a return.
Materials requirement planning	A computer-based production management system that uses sales forecasts to make sure that needed parts and materials are available at the right time and place is referred to as materials requirement planning.
Option	A contract that gives the purchaser the option to buy or sell the underlying financial instrument at a specified price, called the exercise price or strike price, within a specific period of time.
Credibility	The extent to which a source is perceived as having knowledge, skill, or experience relevant to a communication topic and can be trusted to give an unbiased opinion or present objective information on the issue is called credibility.
Warehouse	Warehouse refers to a location, often decentralized, that a firm uses to store, consolidate, age, or mix stock; house product-recall programs; or ease tax burdens.
Data warehouse	A Data warehouse is a repository of integrated information, available for queries and analysis. Data and information are extracted from heterogeneous sources as they are generated.

Management system	A management system is the framework of processes and procedures used to ensure that an organization can fulfill all tasks required to achieve its objectives.
Exchange	The trade of things of value between buyer and seller so that each is better off after the trade is called the exchange.
Protocol	Protocol refers to a statement that, before product development begins, identifies a well-defined target market; specific customers' needs, wants, and preferences; and what the product will be and do.
Performance measurement	The process by which someone evaluates an employee's work behaviors by measurement and comparison with previously established standards, documents the results, and communicates the results to the employee is called performance measurement.
Fund	Independent accounting entity with a self-balancing set of accounts segregated for the purposes of carrying on specific activities is referred to as a fund.
Evaluation	The consumer's appraisal of the product or brand on important attributes is called evaluation.
Corporate goal	A strategic performance target that the entire organization must reach to pursue its vision is a corporate goal.
Stock	In financial terminology, stock is the capital raized by a corporation, through the issuance and sale of shares.
Supply chain management	Supply chain management deals with the planning and execution issues involved in managing a supply chain. Supply chain management spans all movement and storage of raw materials, work-in-process inventory, and finished goods from point-of-origin to point-of-consumption.
Profit	Profit refers to the return to the resource entrepreneurial ability; total revenue minus total cost.
Margin	A deposit by a buyer in stocks with a seller or a stockbroker, as security to cover fluctuations in the market in reference to stocks that the buyer has purchased but for which he has not paid is a margin. Commodities are also traded on margin.
Strategic marketing plan	Strategic marketing plan refers to the planning framework for specific, longtime marketing activities.
Marketing Plan	Marketing plan refers to a road map for the marketing activities of an organization for a specified future period of time, such as one year or five years.
Profit margin	Profit margin is a measure of profitability. It is calculated using a formula and written as a percentage or a number. Profit margin = Net income before tax and interest / Revenue.
Consideration	Consideration in contract law, a basic requirement for an enforceable agreement under traditional contract principles, defined in this text as legal value, bargained for and given in exchange for an act or promise. In corporation law, cash or property contributed to a corporation in exchange for shares, or a promise to contribute such cash or property.
Information system	An information system is a system whether automated or manual, that comprises people, machines, and/or methods organized to collect, process, transmit, and disseminate data that represent user information.
Product line	A group of products that are physically similar or are intended for a similar market are called the product line.
Competitive Strategy	An outline of how a business intends to compete with other firms in the same industry is called competitive strategy.
Audit	An examination of the financial reports to ensure that they represent what they claim and

conform with generally accepted accounting principles is referred to as audit.

Leadership	Management merely consists of leadership applied to business situations; or in other words: management forms a sub-set of the broader process of leadership.
Continuous improvement	The constant effort to eliminate waste, reduce response time, simplify the design of both products and processes, and improve quality and customer service is referred to as continuous improvement.
Process improvement	Process improvement is the activity of elevating the performance of a process, especially that of a business process with regard to its goal.
Preparation	Preparation refers to usually the first stage in the creative process. It includes education and formal training.
Assessment	Collecting information and providing feedback to employees about their behavior, communication style, or skills is an assessment.
Evaluation	The consumer's appraisal of the product or brand on important attributes is called evaluation.
Financial statement	Financial statement refers to a summary of all the transactions that have occurred over a particular period.
Competitor	Other organizations in the same industry or type of business that provide a good or service to the same set of customers is referred to as a competitor.
Consultant	A professional that provides expert advice in a particular field or area in which customers occassionaly require this type of knowledge is a consultant.
Operation	A standardized method or technique that is performed repetitively, often on different materials resulting in different finished goods is called an operation.
Management	Management characterizes the process of leading and directing all or part of an organization, often a business, through the deployment and manipulation of resources. Early twentieth-century management writer Mary Parker Follett defined management as "the art of getting things done through people."
Sales forecasting	Sales forecasting refers to the process of predicting sales of services or goods. The initial step in preparing a master budget.
Realization	Realization is the sale of assets when an entity is being liquidated.
Service	Service refers to a "non tangible product" that is not embodied in a physical good and that typically effects some change in another product, person, or institution. Contrasts with good.
Liaison	An individual who serves as a bridge between groups, tying groups together and facilitating the communication flow needed to integrate group activities is a liaison.
Variance	Variance refers to a measure of how much an economic or statistical variable varies across values or observations. Its calculation is the same as that of the covariance, being the covariance of the variable with itself.
Fiscal year	A fiscal year is a 12-month period used for calculating annual ("yearly") financial reports in businesses and other organizations. In many jurisdictions, regulatory laws regarding accounting require such reports once per twelve months, but do not require that the twelve months constitute a calendar year (i.e. January to December).
Binder	Binder, also called a binding slip, refers to a brief memorandum or agreement issued by an insurer as a temporary policy for the convenience of all the parties, constituting a present insurance in the amount specified, to continue in force until the execution of a formal policy.

Comprehensive	A comprehensive refers to a layout accurate in size, color, scheme, and other necessary details to show how a final ad will look. For presentation only, never for reproduction.
Protocol	Protocol refers to a statement that, before product development begins, identifies a well-defined target market; specific customers' needs, wants, and preferences; and what the product will be and do.
Sales forecast	Sales forecast refers to the maximum total sales of a product that a firm expects to sell during a specified time period under specified environmental conditions and its own marketing efforts.
Purchasing	Purchasing refers to the function in a firm that searches for quality material resources, finds the best suppliers, and negotiates the best price for goods and services.
Production	The creation of finished goods and services using the factors of production: land, labor, capital, entrepreneurship, and knowledge.
Logistics	Those activities that focus on getting the right amount of the right products to the right place at the right time at the lowest possible cost is referred to as logistics.
Marketing	Promoting and selling products or services to customers, or prospective customers, is referred to as marketing.
Hierarchy	A system of grouping people in an organization according to rank from the top down in which all subordinate managers must report to one person is called a hierarchy.
Points	Loan origination fees that may be deductible as interest by a buyer of property. A seller of property who pays points reduces the selling price by the amount of the points paid for the buyer.
Analyst	Analyst refers to a person or tool with a primary function of information analysis, generally with a more limited, practical and short term set of goals than a researcher.
Performance measurement	The process by which someone evaluates an employee's work behaviors by measurement and comparison with previously established standards, documents the results, and communicates the results to the employee is called performance measurement.
Integration	Economic integration refers to reducing barriers among countries to transactions and to movements of goods, capital, and labor, including harmonization of laws, regulations, and standards. Integrated markets theoretically function as a unified market.
Systems design	Systems design is the process or art of defining the hardware and software architecture, components, modules, interfaces, and data for a computer system to satisfy specified requirements.
Case study	A case study is a particular method of qualitative research. Rather than using large samples and following a rigid protocol to examine a limited number of variables, case study methods involve an in-depth, longitudinal examination of a single instance or event: a case. They provide a systematic way of looking at events, collecting data, analyzing information, and reporting the results.
Supply chain	Supply chain refers to the flow of goods, services, and information from the initial sources of materials and services to the delivery of products to consumers.
Inventory	Tangible property held for sale in the normal course of business or used in producing goods or services for sale is an inventory.
Supply	Supply is the aggregate amount of any material good that can be called into being at a certain price point; it comprises one half of the equation of supply and demand. In classical economic theory, a curve representing supply is one of the factors that produce price.

Go to **Cram101.com** for the Practice Tests for this Chapter.

Personnel	A collective term for all of the employees of an organization. Personnel is also commonly used to refer to the personnel management function or the organizational unit responsible for administering personnel programs.
Organizational culture	The mindset of employees, including their shared beliefs, values, and goals is called the organizational culture.
Key Performance Indicator	A Key Performance Indicator is a financial and non-financial metric used to quantify objectives to reflect the strategic performance of an organization.
Senior management	Senior management is generally a team of individuals at the highest level of organizational management who have the day-to-day responsibilities of managing a corporation.
Action plan	Action plan refers to a written document that includes the steps the trainee and manager will take to ensure that training transfers to the job.
Performance improvement	Performance improvement is the concept of measuring the output of a particular process or procedure then modifying the process or procedure in order to increase the output, increase efficiency, or increase the effectiveness of the process or procedure.
Distribution	Distribution in economics, the manner in which total output and income is distributed among individuals or factors.
Distribution center	Designed to facilitate the timely movement of goods and represent a very important part of a supply chain is a distribution center.
Customer service	The ability of logistics management to satisfy users in terms of time, dependability, communication, and convenience is called the customer service.
Knowledge base	Knowledge base refers to a database that includes decision rules for use of the data, which may be qualitative as well as quantitative.
Contribution	In business organization law, the cash or property contributed to a business by its owners is referred to as contribution.

Supply chain	Supply chain refers to the flow of goods, services, and information from the initial sources of materials and services to the delivery of products to consumers.
Raw material	Raw material refers to a good that has not been transformed by production; a primary product.
Service	Service refers to a "non tangible product" that is not embodied in a physical good and that typically effects some change in another product, person, or institution. Contrasts with good.
Supply	Supply is the aggregate amount of any material good that can be called into being at a certain price point; it comprises one half of the equation of supply and demand. In classical economic theory, a curve representing supply is one of the factors that produce price.
Sales forecasting	Sales forecasting refers to the process of predicting sales of services or goods. The initial step in preparing a master budget.
Senior executive	Senior executive means a chief executive officer, chief operating officer, chief financial officer and anyone in charge of a principal business unit or function.
Sales forecast	Sales forecast refers to the maximum total sales of a product that a firm expects to sell during a specified time period under specified environmental conditions and its own marketing efforts.
Corporation	A legal entity chartered by a state or the Federal government that is distinct and separate from the individuals who own it is a corporation. This separation gives the corporation unique powers which other legal entities lack.
Appreciation	Appreciation refers to a rise in the value of a country's currency on the exchange market, relative either to a particular other currency or to a weighted average of other currencies. The currency is said to appreciate. Opposite of 'depreciation.' Appreciation can also refer to the increase in value of any asset.
Business plan	A detailed written statement that describes the nature of the business, the target market, the advantages the business will have in relation to competition, and the resources and qualifications of the owner is referred to as a business plan.
Market	A market is, as defined in economics, a social arrangement that allows buyers and sellers to discover information and carry out a voluntary exchange of goods or services.
Marketing	Promoting and selling products or services to customers, or prospective customers, is referred to as marketing.
Management	Management characterizes the process of leading and directing all or part of an organization, often a business, through the deployment and manipulation of resources. Early twentieth-century management writer Mary Parker Follett defined management as "the art of getting things done through people."
Channel	Channel, in communications (sometimes called communications channel), refers to the medium used to convey information from a sender (or transmitter) to a receiver.
Marketing Plan	Marketing plan refers to a road map for the marketing activities of an organization for a specified future period of time, such as one year or five years.
Consideration	Consideration in contract law, a basic requirement for an enforceable agreement under traditional contract principles, defined in this text as legal value, bargained for and given in exchange for an act or promise. In corporation law, cash or property contributed to a corporation in exchange for shares, or a promise to contribute such cash or property.
Sales management	Planning the selling program and implementing and controlling the personal selling effort of the firm is called sales management.

Go to **Cram101.com** for the Practice Tests for this Chapter.

Accounting	A system that collects and processes financial information about an organization and reports that information to decision makers is referred to as accounting.
Capital	Capital generally refers to financial wealth, especially that used to start or maintain a business. In classical economics, capital is one of four factors of production, the others being land and labor and entrepreneurship.
Profit	Profit refers to the return to the resource entrepreneurial ability; total revenue minus total cost.
Purchasing	Purchasing refers to the function in a firm that searches for quality material resources, finds the best suppliers, and negotiates the best price for goods and services.
Production	The creation of finished goods and services using the factors of production: land, labor, capital, entrepreneurship, and knowledge.
Capital requirement	The capital requirement is a bank regulation, which sets a framework on how banks and depository institutions must handle their capital. The categorization of assets and capital is highly standardized so that it can be risk weighted.
Logistics	Those activities that focus on getting the right amount of the right products to the right place at the right time at the lowest possible cost is referred to as logistics.
Authority	Authority in agency law, refers to an agent's ability to affect his principal's legal relations with third parties. Also used to refer to an actor's legal power or ability to do something. In addition, sometimes used to refer to a statute, case, or other legal source that justifies a particular result.
Credibility	The extent to which a source is perceived as having knowledge, skill, or experience relevant to a communication topic and can be trusted to give an unbiased opinion or present objective information on the issue is called credibility.
Users	Users refer to people in the organization who actually use the product or service purchased by the buying center.
Mentoring	Mentoring refers to a developmental relationship between a more experienced mentor and a less experienced partner referred to as a mentee or protégé. Usually - but not necessarily - the mentor/protégé pair will be of the same sex.
Analyst	Analyst refers to a person or tool with a primary function of information analysis, generally with a more limited, practical and short term set of goals than a researcher.
Financial plan	The financial plan section of a business plan consists of three financial statements (the income statement, the cash flow projection, and the balance sheet) and a brief analysis of these three statements.
Personnel	A collective term for all of the employees of an organization. Personnel is also commonly used to refer to the personnel management function or the organizational unit responsible for administering personnel programs.
Capacity planning	The determination and adjustment of the organization's ability to produce products and services to match customer demand is called capacity planning.
Journal	Book of original entry, in which transactions are recorded in a general ledger system, is referred to as a journal.
Bottleneck	An operation where the work to be performed approaches or exceeds the capacity available to do it is a bottleneck.
Labor	People's physical and mental talents and efforts that are used to help produce goods and services are called labor.

Go to **Cram101.com** for the Practice Tests for this Chapter.

Human resource planning	Forecasting the organization's human resource needs, developing replacement charts for all levels of the organization, and preparing inventories of the skills and abilities individuals need to move within the organization is called human resource planning.
Strategic management	A philosophy of management that links strategic planning with dayto-day decision making. Strategic management seeks a fit between an organization's external and internal environments.
Integration	Economic integration refers to reducing barriers among countries to transactions and to movements of goods, capital, and labor, including harmonization of laws, regulations, and standards. Integrated markets theoretically function as a unified market.
Mistake	In contract law a mistake is incorrect understanding by one or more parties to a contract and may be used as grounds to invalidate the agreement. Common law has identified three different types of mistake in contract: unilateral mistake, mutual mistake, and common mistake.
Manufacturing	Production of goods primarily by the application of labor and capital to raw materials and other intermediate inputs, in contrast to agriculture, mining, forestry, fishing, and services a manufacturing.
Market position	Market position is a measure of the position of a company or product on a market.
Capital planning	Capital planning is an accounting process whereby a financial analyst can determine the economic value of business projects/ventures and allocate capital to those endeavors which present the greatest calculated return on investment.
Collaboration	Collaboration occurs when the interaction between groups is very important to goal attainment and the goals are compatible. Wherein people work together —applying both to the work of individuals as well as larger collectives and societies.
Bottom line	The bottom line is net income on the last line of a income statement.
Firm	An organization that employs resources to produce a good or service for profit and owns and operates one or more plants is referred to as a firm.
Warehouse	Warehouse refers to a location, often decentralized, that a firm uses to store, consolidate, age, or mix stock; house product-recall programs; or ease tax burdens.
Data warehouse	A Data warehouse is a repository of integrated information, available for queries and analysis. Data and information are extracted from heterogeneous sources as they are generated.
Context	The effect of the background under which a message often takes on more and richer meaning is a context. Context is especially important in cross-cultural interactions because some cultures are said to be high context or low context.
Time series	In statistics and signal processing, a time series is a sequence of data points, measured typically at successive times, spaced at (often uniform) time intervals. Analysts throughout the economy will use these to aid in the management of their corresponding businesses.
Competitor	Other organizations in the same industry or type of business that provide a good or service to the same set of customers is referred to as a competitor.
Trend	Trend refers to the long-term movement of an economic variable, such as its average rate of increase or decrease over enough years to encompass several business cycles.
Regression analysis	Regression analysis refers to the statistical technique of finding a straight line that approximates the information in a group of data points. Used throughout empirical economics, including both international trade and finance.
Senior	Senior management is generally a team of individuals at the highest level of organizational

management	management who have the day-to-day responsibilities of managing a corporation.
Assessment	Collecting information and providing feedback to employees about their behavior, communication style, or skills is an assessment.
Policy	Similar to a script in that a policy can be a less than completely rational decision-making method. Involves the use of a pre-existing set of decision steps for any problem that presents itself.
Gap	In December of 1995, Gap became the first major North American retailer to accept independent monitoring of the working conditions in a contract factory producing its garments. Gap is the largest specialty retailer in the United States.
Product manager	Product manager refers to a person who plans, implements, and controls the annual and long-range plans for the products for which he or she is responsible.
Evaluation	The consumer's appraisal of the product or brand on important attributes is called evaluation.
Performance plan	Performance plan refers to an understanding between an employee and a manager concerning what and how a job is to be done such that both parties know what is expected and how success is defined and measured.
Audit	An examination of the financial reports to ensure that they represent what they claim and conform with generally accepted accounting principles is referred to as audit.
Investment	Investment refers to spending for the production and accumulation of capital and additions to inventories. In a financial sense, buying an asset with the expectation of making a return.
Business analysis	Business analysis is a structured methodology that is focused on completely understanding the customer's needs, identifying how best to meet those needs, and then "reinventing" the stream of processes to meet those needs.
Customer service	The ability of logistics management to satisfy users in terms of time, dependability, communication, and convenience is called the customer service.
Operation	A standardized method or technique that is performed repetitively, often on different materials resulting in different finished goods is called an operation.
Shareholder value	For a publicly traded company, shareholder value is the part of its capitalization that is equity as opposed to long-term debt. In the case of only one type of stock, this would roughly be the number of outstanding shares times current shareprice.
Shareholder	A shareholder is an individual or company (including a corporation) that legally owns one or more shares of stock in a joined stock company.
Inventory	Tangible property held for sale in the normal course of business or used in producing goods or services for sale is an inventory.
Total demand	Total demand refers to the demand schedule or the demand curve of all buyers of a good or service; also called market demand.
Carrying cost	The cost to hold an asset, usually inventory is called a carrying cost. For inventory, a carrying cost includes such items as interest, warehousing costs, insurance, and material-handling expenses.
Procurement	Procurement is the acquisition of goods or services at the best possible total cost of ownership, in the right quantity, at the right time, in the right place for the direct benefit or use of the governments, corporations, or individuals generally via, but not limited to a contract.
Distribution	Distribution in economics, the manner in which total output and income is distributed among

individuals or factors.

Incidence	The ultimate economic effect of a tax on the real incomes of producers or consumers. Thus a sales tax may be paid by a retailer, but it is likely that the incidence falls upon the consumer.
Distribution center	Designed to facilitate the timely movement of goods and represent a very important part of a supply chain is a distribution center.
Dividend	Amount of corporate profits paid out for each share of stock is referred to as dividend.
Retained earnings	Cumulative earnings of a company that are not distributed to the owners and are reinvested in the business are called retained earnings.
Working capital	The dollar difference between total current assets and total current liabilities is called working capital.
Fixed capital	Fixed capital is a concept in economics and accounting, first theoretically analysed in some depth by the economist David Ricardo. It refers to any kind of real or physical capital that is not used up in the production of a product. It is contrasted with circulating capital.
Management system	A management system is the framework of processes and procedures used to ensure that an organization can fulfill all tasks required to achieve its objectives.
Demand management	The use of fiscal policy and monetary policy to increase or decrease aggregate demand is called demand management.
Partnership	In the common law, a partnership is a type of business entity in which partners share with each other the profits or losses of the business undertaking in which they have all invested.
Return on investment	Return on investment refers to the return a businessperson gets on the money he and other owners invest in the firm; for example, a business that earned $100 on a $1,000 investment would have a ROI of 10 percent: 100 divided by 1000.

CPSIA information can be obtained at www.ICGtesting.com
Printed in the USA
LVOW10s1320031114

411782LV00002B/39/A

9 781428 812758